Giggle Fit

Silly Knock-Knocks

Illustrated by
Steve Harpster

Joseph
Rosenbloom

Sterling Publishing Co., Inc. New York

Library of Congress Cataloging-in-Publication Data Available

1   3   5   7   9   10   8   6   4   2

Published by Sterling Publishing Company, Inc.
387 Park Avenue South, New York, N.Y. 10016
© 2001 by Joseph Rosenbloom
Distributed in Canada by Sterling Publishing
$^c/_o$ Canadian Manda Group, One Atlantic Avenue, Suite 105
Toronto, Ontario, Canada M6K 3E7
Distributed in Great Britain and Europe by Chris Lloyd at Orca
Book Services, Stanley House, Fleets Lane, Poole BH15 3AJ, England
Distributed in Australia by Capricorn Link (Australia) Pty. Ltd.
P.O. Box 704, Windsor, NSW 2756 Australia
Printed in China

Sterling ISBN 0-8069-8015-X

3 0073 00232 9507

Knock-Knock.
   Who's there?
Afghanistan.
   Afghanistan who?
Afghanistan out here all day.

Knock-Knock.
   Who's there?
Althea.
   Althea who?
Althea later, Alligator!

Knock-Knock.
   Who's there?
Alaska.
   Alaska who?
Alaska my mother.

Knock-Knock.
  Who's there?
Amen.
  Amen who?
Amen hot water again.

Knock-Knock.
  Who's there?
Anita.
  Anita who?
Anita rest.

Knock-Knock.
  Who's there?
Ammonia.
  Ammonia who?
Ammonia a little kid.

Knock-Knock.
Who's there?
Athena.
Athena who?
Athena flying saucer.

Knock-Knock.
Who's there?
Armenia.
Armenia who?
**Armenia every word
I say.**

Knock-Knock.
Who's there?
Avenue.
Avenue who?
**Avenue been missing
me?**

Knock-Knock.
Who's there?
Benny
Benny who?
Benny long time no see.

Knock-Knock.
Who's there?
Banana.

Knock-Knock.
Who's there?
Banana.

Knock-Knock.
Who's there?
Banana.

Knock-Knock.
Who's there?
Orange.
Orange who?
Orange you glad I didn't say Banana?

Knock-Knock.
 Who's there?
Barbie.
 Barbie who?
Barbie Q. Chicken.

Knock-Knock.
 Who's there?
Beth.
 Beth who?
Beth wishes, thweetie.

Knock-Knock.
 Who's there?
Barbara.
 Barbara who?
Barbara black sheep, have you any wool?

Knock-Knock.
　　Who's there?
Budapest.
　　Budapest who?
You're nothing Budapest.

Knock-Knock.
　　Who's there?
Butcher and Jimmy.
　　Butcher and Jimmy who?
Butcher arms around me and Jimmy a little kiss.

Knock-Knock.
   Who's there?
Betty.
   Betty who?
Betty-bye!

Knock-Knock.
   Who's there?
Buck.
   Buck who?
Buck, buck! I'm a chicken!

Knock-Knock.
   Who's there?
Boo.
   Boo who?
Well, you don't have to cry about it.

Knock-Knock.
  Who's there?
Canoe.
  Canoe who?
Canoe please get off my foot?

Knock-Knock.
  Who's there?
Carmen.
  Carmen who?
Carmen get it!

Knock-Knock.
  Who's there?
Catch.
  Catch who?
Bless you!

10

Knock-Knock.
Who's there?
Cher.
Cher who?
Cherlock Holmes.

Knock-Knock.
Who's there?
Cain and Abel.
Cain and Abel who?
Cain talk now, Abel tomorrow.

Knock-Knock.
Who's there?
Celeste.
Celeste who?
Celeste time I'm going to tell you!

Knock-Knock.
  Who's there?
Datsun.
  Datsun who?
Datsun old joke.

Knock-Knock.
  Who's there?
Dexter.
  Dexter who?
Dexter halls with boughs of holly...

Knock-Knock.
  Who's there?
Doughnut.
  Doughnut who?
Doughnut open until Christmas.

Knock-Knock.

Who's there?

Donahue.

Donahue who?

Donahue hide from me, you rat!

Knock-Knock.

Who's there?

Deluxe.

Deluxe who?

Deluxe Ness Monster.

Knock-Knock.

Who's there?

Dishes.

Dishes who?

Dishes the end of the road.

Knock-Knock.
　Who's there?
Danielle.
　Danielle who?
**Danielle — I heard you
the first time.**

　　Knock-Knock.
　　　Who's there?
　　Dora Belle.
　　　Dora Belle who?
　　Dora Belle is broken so I knocked.

　　Knock-Knock.
　　　Who's there?
　　Duane.
　　　Duane who?
　　Duane the bathtub — I'm dwowning.

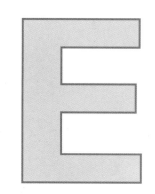

Knock-Knock.
Who's there?
Easter.
Easter who?
Easter anybody home?

Knock-Knock.
Who's there?
Eileen Dunn.
Eileen Dunn who?
Eileen Dunn the doorbell and it broke.

Knock-Knock.
Who's there?
Emerson.
Emerson who?
Emerson nice shoes you've got on.

Knock-Knock.
  Who's there?
Emmet.
  Emmet who?
Emmet your service.

Knock-Knock.
  Who's there?
Ezra.
  Ezra who?
Ezra no hope for me?

Knock-Knock.
  Who's there?
Evan.
  Evan who?
Evan to Betsy!

F

Knock-Knock.
  Who's there?
Franz.
  Franz who?
Franz forever!

Knock-Knock.
  Who's there?
Fido.
  Fido who?
Fido away, will you miss me?

Knock-Knock.
  Who's there?
Fanny.
  Fanny who?
**Fanny-body calls,
I'm out.**

Knock-Knock.
   Who's there?
Flea.
   Flea who?
Flea blind mice.

Knock-Knock.
   Who's there?
Freddie.
   Freddie who?
Freddie or not, here I come.

Knock-Knock.
   Who's there?
Fletcher.
   Fletcher who?
Fletcher self go.

Knock-Knock.
    Who's there?
Gladys.
    Gladys who?
Gladys see you.

Knock-Knock.
    Who's there?
Goat.
    Goat who?
Goat to your room.

Knock-Knock.
    Who's there?
Gopher.
    Gopher who?
Gopher the gold!

Knock-Knock.
  Who's there?
Goliath.
  Goliath who?
Goliath down and go to sleep!

Knock-Knock.
  Who's there?
Greta.
  Greta who?
You Greta my nerves!

Knock-Knock.
  Who's there?
Gorilla.
  Gorilla who?
Gorilla cheese sandwich.

Knock-Knock.
  Who's there?
Gideon.
  Gideon who?
Gideon your horse and let's go!

Knock-Knock.
  Who's there?
Gus.
  Gus who?
That's what you're supposed to do.

H

Knock-Knock.
Who's there?
Harvey.
Harvey who?
Harvey having fun yet?

Knock-Knock.
Who's there?
Howell.
Howell who?
**Howell you have your pizza,
plain or with sausage?**

Knock-Knock.
Who's there?
Hawaii.
Hawaii who?
I'm fine, how are you?

Knock-Knock.
   Who's there?
Hammond.
   Hammond who?
Hammond eggs.

Knock-Knock.
   Who's there?
Hugo.
   Hugo who?
Hugo your way and I'll go mine.

Knock-Knock.
   Who's there?
Hannah.
   Hannah who?
Hannah partridge in a pear tree.

Knock-Knock.

Who's there?

Iguana.

Iguana who?

Iguana hold your hand.

Knock-Knock.

Who's there?

Irish stew.

Irish stew who?

Irish stew would come out and play.

Knock-Knock.

Who's there?

Isabella.

Isabella who?

Isabella out of order?

Knock-Knock.

Who's there?

Izzy.

Izzy who?

Izzy come, Izzy go.

Knock-Knock.
Who's there?
Juno.
Juno who?
Juno what time it is?

Knock-Knock.
Who's there?
Justin.
Justin who?
Justin time for dinner.

Knock-Knock.
Who's there?
Jupiter.
Jupiter who?
Jupiter fly in my soup?

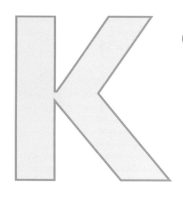

Knock-Knock.
 Who's there?
Kenny.
 Kenny who?
Kenny stay for dinner if he calls his mom?

Knock-Knock.
 Who's there?
Kareem.
 Kareem who?
Kareem of wheat.

Knock-Knock.
 Who's there?
Kimona.
 Kimona who?
Kimona my house.

Knock-Knock.
 Who's there?
Keith.
 Keith who?
Keith me, you fool.

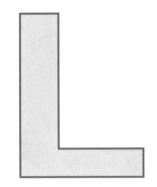

Knock-Knock.
 Who's there?
Little old lady.
 Little old lady who?
I didn't know you could yodel.

Knock-Knock.
 Who's there?
Lion.
 Lion who?
Lion here on your doorstep till you open the door.

Knock-Knock.
 Who's there?
Lauren.
 Lauren who?
Lauren order.

Knock-Knock.
Who's there?
Lettuce.

Lettuce who?
**Lettuce in and we'll tell
    you another knock-
    knock joke.**

Knock-Knock.
    Who's there?
Luke.
    Luke who?
Luke before you leap.

Knock-Knock.
    Who's there?
Lois.
    Lois who?
Lois man on the totem pole.

Knock-Knock.
Who's there?
Megan, Elise, and Chicken.
Megan, Elise, and Chicken who?
Megan, Elise — and Chicken it twice, gonna find out who's naughty and nice...

Knock-Knock.
Who's there?
Mandy.
Mandy who?
Mandy lifeboats — the ship's sinking!

Knock-Knock.
Who's there?
Marmalade.
Marmalade who?
"Marmalade an egg," said the little chicken.

N

Knock-Knock.
  Who's there?
Nona.
  Nona who?
Nona your business.

Knock-Knock.
  Who's there?
  Needle.
    Needle who?
  Needle little lunch.

Knock-Knock.
  Who's there?
Nana.
  Nana who?
Nana your business.

Knock-Knock.
　Who's there?
Nettie.
　Nettie who?
Nettie as a fruit-cake.

Knock-Knock.
　Who's there?
Nadya.
　Nadya who?
Nadya head if you understand what I'm saying.

Knock-Knock.
　Who's there?
N. E.
　N. E. who?
N. E. body home?

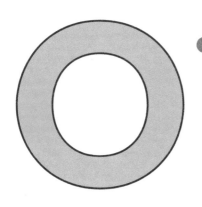

Knock-Knock.
  Who's there?
Oink oink.
  Oink oink who?
Are you a pig or an owl?

Knock-Knock.
  Who's there?
Olivia.
  Olivia who?
Olivia me alone!

Knock-Knock.
  Who's there?
Omar.
  Omar who?
Omar goodness gracious — wrong door!

Knock-Knock.
  Who's there?
Oscar and Greta.
  Oscar and Greta who?
Oscar foolish question, and Greta a foolish answer.

Knock-Knock.
  Who's there?
Ohio.
  Ohio who?
Ohio Silver!

Knock-Knock.
  Who's there?
Omega.
  Omega who?
Omega up your mind.

Knock-Knock.
Who's there?
Police.
Police who?
Police open the door.

Knock-Knock.
Who's there?
Philippa.
Philippa who?
Philippa bathtub, I'm dirty.

Knock-Knock.
Who's there?
Pasta.
Pasta who?
Pasta pizza.

Knock-Knock.
   Who's there?
Queen.
   Queen who?
Queen up your room.

Knock-Knock.
   Who's there?
Quacker.
   Quacker who?
Quacker nother bad joke and I'm leaving.

Knock-Knock.
   Who's there?
Quebec.
   Quebec.
Quebec to the end of the line.

Knock-Knock.
Who's there?
Rocky.
Rocky who?
Rocky-bye baby, on the treetop...

Knock-Knock.
Who's there?
Rhoda.
Rhoda who?
Rhoda boat.

Knock-Knock.
Who's there?
Ringo.
Ringo who?
Ringo round the collar.

Knock-Knock.
Who's there?
Raven.
Raven who?
Raven maniac.

Knock-Knock.
   Who's there?
Sancho.
   Sancho who?
Sancho a letter but you never answered.

Knock-Knock.
   Who's there?
Siam.
   Siam who?
Siam your old pal.

Knock-Knock.
   Who's there?
Schick.
   Schick who?
Schick as a dog.

Knock-Knock.
Who's there?
Sarah.
Sarah who?
Sarah doctor in the house?

Knock-Knock.
Who's there?
Siamese.
Siamese who?
Siamese-y to please.

Knock-Knock.
Who's there?
Senior.
Senior who?
**Senior through the keyhole, so
I know you're in there.**

Knock-Knock.
  Who's there?
Theresa.
  Theresa who?
Theresa fly in my soup.

Knock-Knock.
  Who's there?
Toothache.
  Toothache who?
Toothache the high road and I'll take the low road....

Knock-Knock.
  Who's there?
Trigger.
  Trigger who?
Trigger treat!

Knock-Knock.
Who's there?
Unaware.
Unaware who?
Unaware is what you put on first in the morning.

Knock-Knock.
Who's there?
Uganda.
Uganda who?
Uganda lot of weight.

Knock-Knock.
Who's there?
Unity.
Unity who?
Unity sweater for me?

Knock-Knock.
 Who's there?
Venice.
 Venice who?
Venice lunch?

Knock-Knock.
 Who's there?
Vanessa.
 Vanessa who?
Vanessa you going to grow up?

Knock-Knock.
 Who's there?
Vilma.
 Vilma who?
**Vilma frog turn into
a prince?**

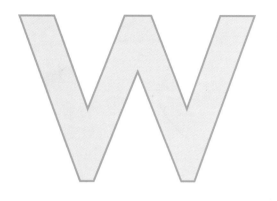

Knock-Knock.
  Who's there?
Weasel.
  Weasel who?
Weasel while you work...

Knock-Knock.
  Who's there?
Weirdo.
  Weirdo who?
Weirdo you think you're going?

Knock-Knock.
  Who's there?
Wendy Katz.
  Wendy Katz who?
**Wendy Katz away,
the mice will play.**

Knock-Knock.
  Who's there?
Willoughby.
  Willoughby who?
Willoughby my valentine?

Knock-Knock.
  Who's there?
Willie.
  Willie who?
Willie or won't he?

Knock-Knock.
  Who's there?
Will you remember me in a week?
  Yes.
Will you remember me in a month?
  Yes.
Will you remember me in a year?
  Yes.
Will you remember me in five years?
  Yes.
Knock-Knock.
  Who's there?
See? You've forgotten me already!

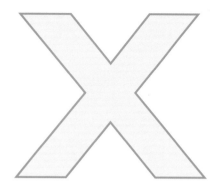

Knock-Knock.
Who's there?
Xavier breath.
Xavier breath who?
Xavier breath — I'm not listening.

Knock-Knock.
Who's there?
X.
X who?
X for breakfast.

Knock-Knock.
Who's there?
X.
X who?
X me no questions, I'll tell you no lies.

Knock-Knock.
　Who's there?
Yah.
　　Yah who?
Ride 'em, cowboy!

Knock-Knock.
　Who's there?
Yachts.
　　Yachts who?
Yachts new?

Knock-Knock.
　Who's there?
Yule.
　　Yule who?
Yule be sorry!

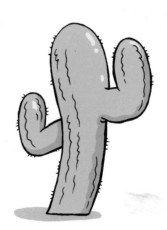

Knock-Knock.
  Who's there?
Yeti.
  Yeti who?
Yeti nother knock-knock joke.

Knock-Knock.
  Who's there?
Yuma.
  Yuma who?
Yuma best friend.

Knock-Knock.
  Who's there?
Yule.
  Yule who?
Yule never guess.

Knock-Knock.
  Who's there?
Zipper.
  Zipper who?
Zipper dee-doo-dah!

Knock-Knock.
  Who's there?
Zizi.
  Zizi who?
Zizi when you know how.

Knock-Knock.
  Who's there?
Zoe.
  Zoe who?
Zoe have come to the end of the book!

INDEX